Gaga for Googles!

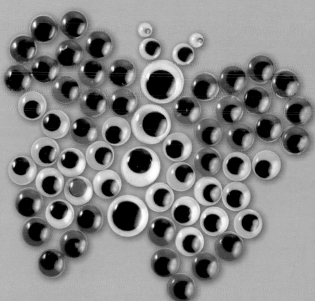

Programming

Quarto is the authority on a wide range of topics.
Quarto educates, entertains and enriches the lives of our readers—
enthusiasts and lovers of hands-on living.
www.quartoknows.com

Crafts by Heidi Fiedler, Pauline Molinari, Rae Siebels,
Pam Thompson, Jenna Winterberg, and Laurie Young.
Illustrations by Adrian D'Alimonte.
Instructional illustrations by Diana Fisher.
Written by Samantha Chagollan and Julie Chapa.
Page Layout by Malik Calimbas.

6 Orchard Road, Suite 100
Lake Forest, CA 92630
quartoknows.com
Visit our blogs @quartoknows.com

Printed in China
1 3 5 7 9 10 8 6 4 2
1967

Introduction

Getting Started With Googly Eyes

What is a googly eye?
A googly eye is a small (and sometimes colorful) bit of plastic that can bring anything to life. With a couple of googly eyes, you can turn rocks into pets, ordinary sunglasses into a fashion statement, and office supplies into newfound friends. Within these pages are tons of things to make and do with these amazing googly eyes, including games to play, crafts to create, and silly puns to make your friends giggle. And when you're done with these ideas, chances are you'll come up with more of your own. The possibilities are endless!

Each idea uses different materials: Craft glue, felt, pom-poms...you name it! You probably already have a lot of these crafting materials at home, and any supplies you don't have can be found at your local craft store. Remember, anything you do with googly eyes is going to require one very important tool: your imagination!

Don't keep the googly fun all to yourself!
Have googly-eyed get-togethers with your friends, or invite your parents to join in on the fun (especially if something seems hard to do on your own).

Above all, have fun!

All Hands on Desk

Q: My mom says someone should keep an eye on me. What does that mean?

A: Maybe you just need someone to keep you company while you do your homework. How about some desk pals?

Paper Clip Pals

Q: How can I give my homework some extra pizzazz?

A: Create a paper clip buddy to give your reports some personality!

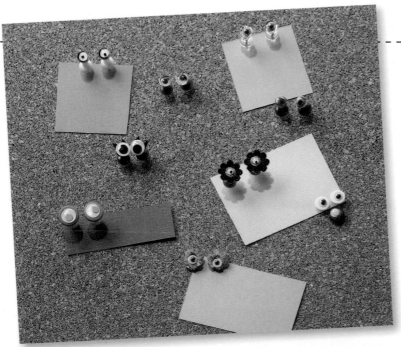

Eye See Your Point

These colorful pushpins are made even cuter by their googly-eyed decorations!

Snake Eyes

This slithery snake makes a great hand warmer for those cold nights.

Supplies needed:
- fabric
- scissors
- glue
- uncooked rice
- felt
- googly eyes

Instructions:

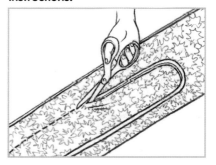

1. Cut two long oval-shaped pieces of fabric.

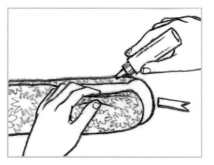

2. Glue the fabric together, folding the edges under. Leave one end open, and attach the tongue to the bottom layer.

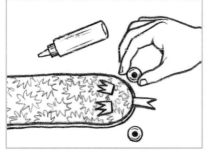

3. Fill with rice, and glue the opening closed. Glue on felt eyelashes and googly eyes.

Pencil Pets

Glue a piece of faux marabou or a pom-pom to the top of your pencil. Add googly eyes, and you've got a new friend!

5

Charming Cups

Take paper tags (found at office supply stores), and add a funny face. Add a split ring, and poke through a plastic cup for a truly charming drink!

Eye-full Tower

Ah, Paris, the city of love...and home to the Eiffel Tower, where millions of tourists go every year to gaze at this amazing sight. What's that, you say? You've never seen it? Well make your own!

Instructions:
Trace the template on this page onto cardstock. Then cut it out and fill it with googly eyes. Now you can gaze upon your own "Eye-full" Tower!

Takin' the Red Eye

One direct flight, coming your way!
For a real red-eye flight, make a paper
airplane out of red paper; add red
eyes, and let it fly!

Butterfly Eye Mosaic

Create beautiful mosaic art! Outline a
butterfly shape, and fill in the wings with
googlies of different sizes and colors.
Try using googlies to make
other cool mosaics!

Googly Frame

Show off your favorite selfie in this
wacky googly eye frame!

Flip & Flop

Q: How can I make my flip-flops more fun?

A: Add googly eyes, of course! Just one extra-large googly is all you need for each shoe. Then you'll be flip-flopping in style!

Eye See the Light

Lighten up! Give your light switch cover a real eye-opening addition—a pair of googlies!

I Have Eyes on the Back of My Head!

Well, actually, it's a barrette. But we won't tell anyone if you won't. Take a regular barrette, and add a pair of large googly eyes. For a furrier feel, add some faux feathers!

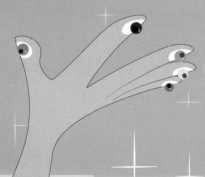

Finger & Toe Nail Decals

From fingertip to toenail, wow 'em with an "eye-deal" manicure or pedicure. Just use a bit of nail polish to attach an eye to each nail!

Kissable Kritters

Give sweet treats some personality!
Trace the template below onto fabric or cardstock.
Then glue together the edges and place on top of a
chocolate treat. Wait—don't forget the googly eyes!

Template

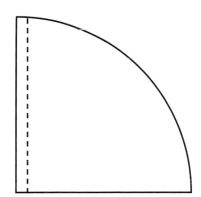

Egg-cellent Pals

Q: What do you call a
mischievous egg?

A: A practical yolker!

Add googly eyes and
other decorations to
plastic eggs to create
these fun and funky
little containers.

9

Eye-Love-You Card

Tell someone how you feel about them with this quirky card.

Supplies needed:
- cardstock
- pencil
- scissors
- black marker
- glue
- large googly eye
- foam hearts
- letter U sticker

Instructions:

1. Fold the cardstock in half. Draw an eye shape on the front of the card, and cut it out. Trace the edges with black marker.

2. Glue the eye in the center of the opening. Close the card, and glue on the foam hearts.

3. Apply the letter U sticker. Don't have a letter U sticker? Use your marker to draw it!

My Eyes Are Glued to This Letter

Want a unique way to seal that note?
Add some glitter glue and a pair of eyes!

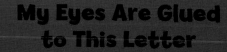

Loaded Dice

Load up a pair of foam cubes with googly eyes of all shapes and sizes!

Sock It To Me

These socks are a sight for sore eyes! Some socks already have goofy creatures on 'em—all you have to do is add googly eyes to make 'em even goofier!

Hop to it!

Hop to it!

Playful Puppets

Talk with your hands! Start with a glove or a mitten, add googly eyes, felt, and yarn, and you've got a puppet parade!

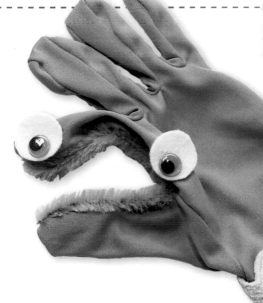

Pom-Pom Pals

Alien? Monster? Harmless puffy friend?
The choice is yours!

Cute Caterpillar

Before a butterfly grows up, it's a caterpillar...
Create your own caterpillar by twisting a green
pipe cleaner and adding a pair of googly eyes!

Colorful Butterfly

Did you know that a butterfly's eye is
about 100 times less accurate than a
human's? So give this butterfly made of
colorful craft sticks a handful of extra
eyes—maybe it will help!

Fishy Friends

Q: What do you call a fish
with no eyes?
A: Fsh!

Supplies needed:
- craft foam
- scissors
- glitter glue
- two old CDs
- glue
- googly eyes
- fishing line

Instructions:

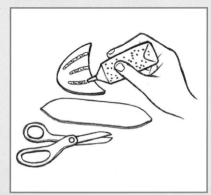

1. Cut craft foam pieces for the tail. Add glitter glue to the tail, and let dry. Cut one longer piece of foam for the fins, and set aside.

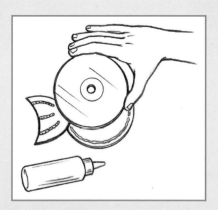

2. With the tail sandwiched between the disks, glue the CDs together, with the colorful side out. Allow it to dry.

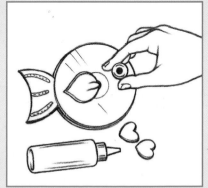

3. Push the fin piece through the hole in the center. Add googly eyes and heart-shaped lips. Loop fishing line through the middle to hang.

13

Rest Your Eyes

Uninterrupted beauty rest! Behind the mask, you can take a blissful nap.

Make your own!
Take a simple sleeping mask, and add glitter, glue, and googly eyes to glam it up. Don't forget eyelashes and a beauty mark!

Superhero Mask

With this mask, you can save the world! At least in your dreams. Add some googlies and heroic decorations to a sleeping mask to conquer evil villains.

Eye-rings

Q: What do you get when you wear
googly eyes on your ears?
A: An earful of compliments!

Make your own! Use craft glue to attach
a pair of googly eyes to earring backs
(found at your local craft store).

Have You Seen My Ring?

Everyone will want a look at this jewelry!
Add an eye or two for a ring that just
screams "Look at me!"

Watch This!

Use craft glue to attach googly eyes to a
black watchband for timely fashion.

Have You Seen My Headband?

Q: I've heard people use the phrase "in my mind's eye."
Does your mind really have an eye?
A: Well, not an actual eye, like the kind that has eyelashes.
But you can have an extra pair on your head if you glue
some googly eyes to a headband!

Bottle-holder Buddies

Need someone to remind you to drink your water?
Create a googly-eyed bottle buddy
to remind you to quench your thirst!

Supplies needed:
- water bottle
- thin and wide ribbon
- craft glue
- silk flower
- pom-pom
- googly eyes

Instructions:

1. Start by cutting a piece of thin ribbon that's long enough to go around your water bottle, and create a handle. Glue both ends to the bottom of the bottle.

2. Wrap thicker ribbon around the middle (over the thinner ribbon), and glue in place.

3. Glue on a silk flower, a pom-pom, and a pair of googly eyes to complete your bottle buddy.

16

Eye'll Keep Your Place

Mark your spot! With a little craft foam and some googly eyes, you can make a truly magnetic bookmark!

Instructions:

1. Cut a piece of foam 2" wide and 2" longer than the length of your book. Crease the foam 2" down from the top edge. Attach four small magnets as shown.

2. Decorate the flap with craft foam designs and googly eyes!

Rock On...

With your own pet rock band!

Supplies needed:
- rocks with flat bottoms
- pipe cleaners
- felt
- faux fur
- old bottle caps
- stickers

Instructions:

1. Find at least three rocks that have flat bottoms (so they can stand up straight). Add googly eyes.

2. Use pipe cleaners, faux fur, or decorative trim to create rockin' hairstyles. Don't forget to accessorize!

3. Use old bottle caps for instruments! To make drums, glue bottle caps to pom-poms. To make a guitar, glue a pipe cleaner to the bottom of the bottle cap.

17

M'eye Mandala

Q: What's a mandala?
A: The word mandala means "circle" in the Sanskrit language (from India). Mandalas are symbolic patterns that are often made with a circle divided into sections.

Traditionally, mandalas are created with colored sand, but you can also use markers, glitter glue, colored pencils, or even googly eyes!

Supplies needed:
- paper
- pencil
- cardstock
- glue
- colored sand
- googly eyes

Instructions:

1. Draw a mandala design on paper. You can trace one from the opposite page or create your own.

2. Turn your design over, and rub the back with a pencil.

3. Turn the design over, and place it on top of the cardstock. Trace over your design again.

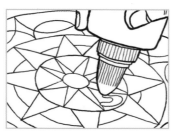

4. The design is now on the cardstock. Evenly apply glue to your design, one area at a time.

5. While the glue is still wet, apply colored sand to your design.

6. Allow the glue to dry, and then shake off any excess sand. Now add some googly eyes!

Templates

Bloomin' Eyes

Ever heard of a plant that keeps a watchful eye on you? This one keeps a lot of eyes on you! Just add googlies to any silk plant for this eye-popping effect!

Plants with Personality

The plants have eyes! Glue a pair of eyes to your favorite pot, and use paint or markers to create a funny face. Finish it off by using the plant as "hair."

Prickly Stares

You've heard of goose bumps, right? Sometimes you get them when someone is staring at the back of your head. Maybe someone like...a cactus with eyes?

Keep an Eye on My Plant

Plants get lonely too. Make a friend for yours with a plastic spoon and some googly eyes.

Handy Hedgehog

This particular hedgehog makes a nice pencil holder, and he's kind of fun to look at too.

Supplies needed:
- air-dry clay in various colors
- small glass bottle
- pencils
- googly eyes

Instructions:

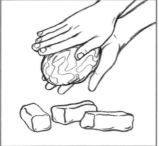

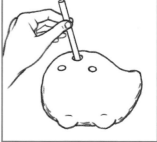

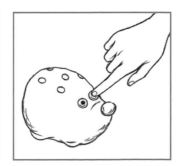

1. Roll different colors of clay together to create a marbled effect.

2. Press clay around the bottle, and shape into a ball. Add a piece of black clay for the nose and four pieces for the feet.

3. Insert pencils into the clay to create holes for the "quills," but remove the pencils until the clay is dry.

4. Press googly eyes firmly into the clay. Let dry completely before reinserting the pencils.

Tinfoil Aliens

Create some out-of-this-world pals!

Supplies needed:
- tinfoil
- pipe cleaners
- googly eyes
- glue

Instructions:

1. Crumple the tinfoil into any shape for the body.

2. Cut and bend the pipe cleaners to make arms and legs.

3. Glue the pipe-cleaner arms and legs to the tinfoil.

4. Add googly eyes!

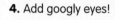

Cartoon Puzzle People

Use some old puzzle pieces to make your own cartoon characters! Use a marker to draw hair, clothes, and smiles on the back side of the puzzle piece. Don't forget to add the googly eyes!

Lollipop Ghosts

Knock, knock.
Who's there?
Boo.
Boo who?
Don't cry your eyes out— here's a lollipop!

Eye Candy

Start with a plastic cup. For the pirate-worthy booty pictured here, add one googly eye, one patch, one felt mouth, and one strip of a bandanna. Add pipe cleaners for the patch strap, and use two twisted together for the handle. Don't forget the loot!

23

Spooky Spider

All you need for this creepy-crawly creature is a couple of pom-poms, some pipe cleaners, and a pair of googly eyes. Glue a small pom-pom onto a large pom-pom. Bend and attach pipe cleaners, and add some googly eyes.

Template

Spin a web!

Just fold a square piece of paper in half to create a triangle, and then fold it again to create a smaller triangle. Make several cuts along the long edge of the triangle, following the guidelines at the left. Round the corners to finish.

Evil Eye Headband

Is someone staring you down? Give 'em the evil eye right back. Attach one large and several small googlies to a headband, and then turn it on anyone who dares to eyeball you.

Angel vs. Devil Salt & Pepper

Q: Why would I make these?
A: To make your food more heavenly or tempting!

Eye Matey

Are you the leader of your pack?
Show them who's captain—make like a pirate
and wear an eye patch! Arrgh!

Money Monster

This creature eats your money! Well, okay, he'll give
it back if you're nice. Just add eyes to any coin purse
to make your own money monster!

Perfect Pumpkins

Q: My pumpkin lacks personality.
How can I give it something extra?
A: Googly eyes make all the difference!
Turn your pumpkin into a pretty princess
or a punky pirate—just make it googly!

Pillow Monsters

There's nothing scary about these monstrously cute pillows! With a needle and thread, some felt, and a pair of googly eyes, you can make your own mini monsters too.

Supplies needed:
- paper
- pencil
- felt
- embroidery thread
- needle
- pillow stuffing
- googly eyes
- fabric glue

Instructions:

1. Draw your own unique monster design on paper. Trace the shape of the monster on two layers of felt, and cut them out.

2. Sew the pieces together, leaving a small section open. Fill with pillow stuffing, and then stitch up the hole.

3. Add googly eyes and felt features; secure with fabric glue.

Simple sewing tips:

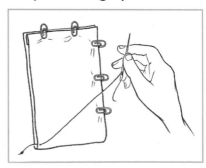

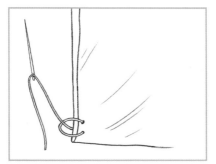

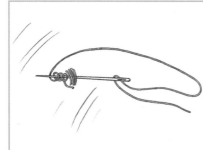

Getting started
1. Hold the two pieces of your design in place with paper clips. Thread the needle, knotting one end. Poke the needle between the two layers and pull through until the knot catches.

Stitching
2. Now push the needle through both layers close to the first stitch. Pull until there is a small loop. Stitch through the loop, and pull tight to create a knot.

Knotting
3. To tie off, slip the needle through your last stitches. Wrap the thread around the needle and pull the needle through.

Talkin' Turkey

Bet the pilgrims wished they had these!
These turkeys may not have been at the first
Thanksgiving dinner, but they can be at yours!

Supplies needed:
- pom-poms
- glue
- scissors
- craft foam
- googly eyes
- feathers
- cardstock
- stick-on letters

Instructions:

1. Glue two pom-poms together. Using the template to the right, cut out the feet and beak from craft foam and glue them on.

2. Glue on googly eyes and feathers for the tail.

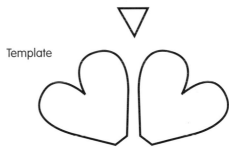

Template

Eye Found a Friend

Q: I found a really cool leaf on a hike the other day. I'd hate to throw it away, but what can I do with it?
A: Nature is our friend, you know. Add googly eyes, and turn your found leaf into a natural companion!

27

All Eyes on the Christmas Tree

Create these masked ornaments to decorate your Christmas tree. These heroes will guard the gifts from being stolen by villains!

Supplies needed:
- bulb ornaments
- felt
- scissors
- glue
- googly eyes

Instructions:

1. Cut out a mask shape from the felt. Make sure it wraps all the way around the bulb ornament!

2. Glue the felt mask to the bulb, and glue googly eyes in the eye holes.

See This? It's a Gift!

Who needs boring gift wrap and a bow?
A googly-eyed gift is so much better.
Wrap a present in polka-dot paper, and then
add googly eyes to create a pretty package.

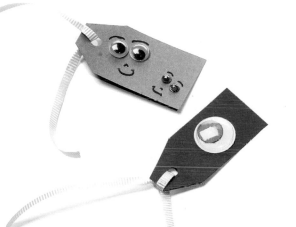

Tag! You're It!

Nothing says "It's from me" better
than a googly gift tag!
Add eyes of all sizes and colors to make
your own cool designs on gift tags.

Candy Cane Reindeer

Create your own festive candy canes! Take
a brown pipe cleaner and twist it around the
bend of the candy cane. Glue some googly
eyes and a pom-pom nose to the front!

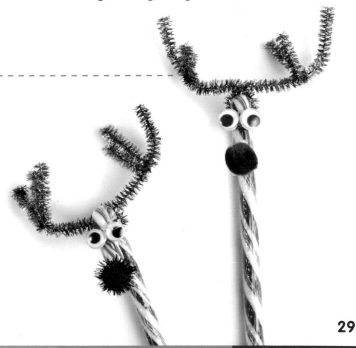

29

Thumbprint Critters

Q: Help! I've got ink on my thumb.
What do I do?
A: Get creative! Grab a pencil or pen and some googly eyes to make a crop of colorful critters.

Beady-eyed Bobbles

Need a fun desk pal? Make a beady-eyed bobble—it's sure to make you giggle! Just use wooden beads, googly eyes, and coiled craft wire to create your own bobble pal. Add felt, foam, or feathers if you want!

Pudgy Piggy

Stash your cash!
Start by finding a plain white clay piggy bank, paint it pink, and embellish with googly eyes.
Then start saving!

Socked-in Snowman

Q: It's July, but I miss wintertime and snowball fights. What can I do?
A: You can make sock snowmen any time of the year!

Supplies needed:
- small white sock
- uncooked rice
- small rubber bands
- glue
- googly eyes
- buttons or beads
- ribbon
- pom-poms
- twigs or pipe cleaners
- scissors

Instructions:

1. Pour rice into the sock, and create body sections by wrapping rubber bands around the middle. Leave at least 1" at the top.

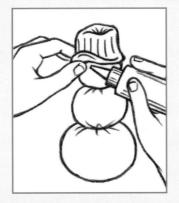

2. Secure a third rubber band around the top of the sock tightly; pull the top of the sock back down over the top to make a hat. Glue it in place.

3. Glue on googly eyes and other details to create the nose, mouth, and buttons. Tie a ribbon around the neck for the scarf, and top the hat with a pom-pom.

4. Poke two small twigs or pipe cleaners into the middle section for the arms. (If the socks are thick, use your scissors to poke a hole through the material first.)

Eye Spy

Q: My best friend is at my house, and we're bored. What's a new game we can play?

A: While your friend isn't watching, make an "Eye Spy" jar, filling it with a bunch of random stuff from your house. Make a list of everything you put in it.

Now show the jar to your friend for 15 seconds, and then put it away. Ask your friend to write down everything she saw in the jar. Compare the two lists to see how many things she was able to remember. The best part about this game? You can change the jar's contents after each game, so no two games are ever the same!

Tic-Tac-Eye

Jazz up this popular game! Glue strips of funky fabric to cardstock for the Xs, and glue large googlies to card stock for the Os. Let the games begin!

Clothespin Art Critics

Give your latest masterpiece rave reviews! Use googly eyes, clothespins, fabric, pipe cleaners, craft wire, and decorative trims to create these fancy clips—and then use them to hang up your favorite artwork! (Pay no attention if they roll their eyes—not everyone appreciates the classics!)

Eye'm Ready for My Close-up

Magnetize your favorite photos. Cut out the faces from your favorite goofy shots, add paper clothes and bodies, and glue a magnet to the back. Don't forget the googly eyes!

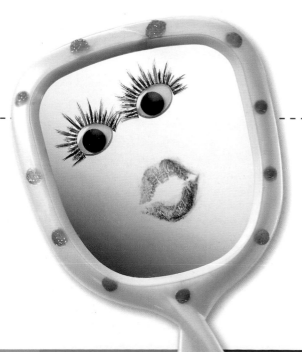

Here's Looking at You, Kid

Q: Whose face is that in the mirror?
A: It's yours, of course!
But you can be sure you'll always have a happy reflection if you add a fun face to your mirror.

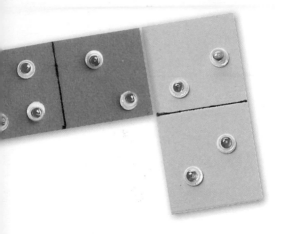

Dotty Dominoes

Cut 28 pieces of craft foam into small rectangles. Draw a line across the middle of each piece. Add up to six googly eyes to each square, and leave some squares empty. Each domino should be different. Now have fun playing!

Doggie Bags

Spice up your lunch—or your pooch's! A simple brown bag looks so much cuter with some googly eyes and a little art!

Doggie's Travel Bag

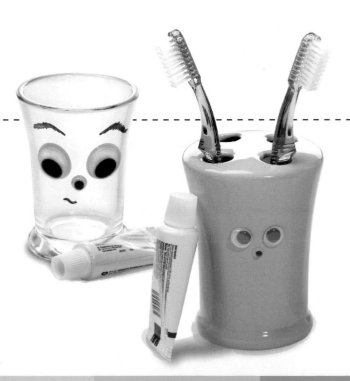

Bathroom Buddies

Everyone likes a friendly face first thing in the morning—and these bathroom buddies won't let you down!

Food Preservers

Q: How can I make
my lunch more exciting?
A: Try using a food container
with personality! Use craft foam
to create a pet portrait. Then add
pop-poms, felt, and googly eyes.

Supplies needed:
- reusable food container
- craft foam
- felt
- pom-poms
- googly eyes
- glue
- scissors

Instructions:

1. Cut out the shape of a dog or a cat face.
Make sure the shape isn't too big or too small
to fit on the lid!

2. Cut out shapes for the ears, nose, collar, and any other decorations.

3. Glue the face to the lid along with the ears, nose, and collar.

4. Glue other decorations to finish the face. Don't forget the googly eyes!

Picture This!

Display your favorite pix!
Craft a funky cat, an outrageous octopus,
or a creepy-crawly spider to store
notes and show off photos!

Super Sock Creature

This friendly face is sure to cheer up any grump!
With a few simple supplies, you can create your own sock buddy!

Supplies needed:
- knee-high sock
- pillow stuffing
- yarn
- glue
- foam flowers
- scissors
- pipe cleaners
- pom-poms
- googly eyes

Instructions:

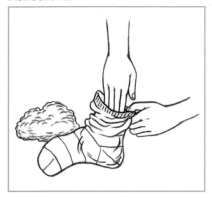

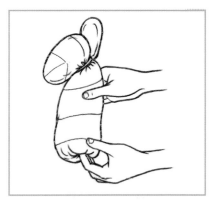

1. Stuff the foot of the sock with pillow stuffing until firm. (The foot of the sock will become your creature's head, and the toe of the sock will be its chin.)

2. Tie a knot around the neck with a piece of yarn. Fill the leg of the sock with more stuffing.

3. Tie a knot with another piece of yarn at the top of the sock to close It up. Now push the end of the sock up inside the body.

4. Squish the stuffing around in the body until it's steady enough to stand. Glue two foam flowers to the base for feet.

5. Glue foam flowers to two pipe cleaners for the hands. Glue the stems at the back of the body; glue one more flower over that to cover it.

6. Add pom-poms and googly eyes for the face; use small foam flowers for eyelashes.

Origami Zoo

It's a whale of a craft! Origami is the art of folded paper—and with googly eyes, these origami creatures really come to life!

Make a zoo full of paper pals! Check out an origami book from the library, or look online for more origami animal ideas and patterns.

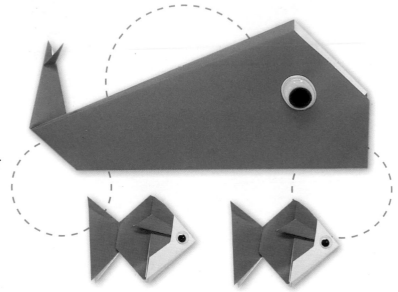

Instructions:

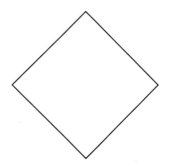

1. Start with a square sheet of colored paper.

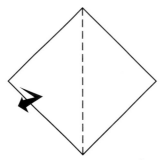

2. Fold the right point over the left to make a center crease. Unfold.

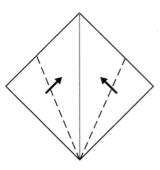

3. Fold the lower right and lower left sides to meet at the center crease.

4. It looks like a kite. Now fold the top point down to meet the corners.

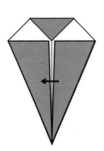

5. Fold the right side over the left along the center crease.

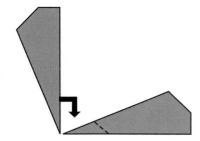

6. Turn 90 degrees, and fold up the end point to make a tail. Add googlies!

Googly Glasses

Q: Why is everyone staring at me?
A: They're jealous of your new funky sunglasses. What an eyeful!

More Than Meets the Eye

This is no ordinary bracelet!
The googly eyes may look like unusual jewels
at first glance, but look closer for a real eyeful!

Eye-deal Shoes

These are sure to make your fancy feet a real shoe-in for the "Most Creative Dresser" award! Glue googly eyes, silk flowers, pom-poms, pipe cleaners, sequins, or anything else you like on your shoes to give them some real "face value."

Eye C U!

Magnetic Fun!
Add eyes, beads, and some glitter glue to magnets to create funny faces.

Eye Glass

Q: Why do I feel like I'm always being watched?
A: Because there are eyes all over your favorite drinking glass, silly!

Wand-ering Eye

This wacky wand may not make your wishes come true, but it will surely turn all eyes on you! Grab a plain dowel rod, and tie colorful ribbons on the end. Finish it off by gluing a huge googly eye on the top!

Eye Luv Flowers

Stash your glasses with style! Glue googly eyes to self-adhesive craft-foam flowers, and decorate a plastic case for your glasses. Add rhinestones for extra sparkle!

Egg-carton Caterpillar

Q: What can I do with an old egg carton?
A: Make your own crafty caterpillar!

Supplies needed:
- egg carton
- paint
- pipe cleaners
- googly eyes
- glue
- scissors

Instructions:

1. Cut the egg carton into one row. Make it as long as you'd like!

2. Paint the egg carton the color you want your caterpillar to be, and allow it to dry.

3. Glue pipe cleaners to the bottom for feet, and add googly eyes!

Shake It, Don't Break It

Googly eyes make a great sound! Throw them in a toilet paper roll for an instant shaker, or use an old chip container—then when you're done, you can use it to store your extra googlies!

Supplies needed:
- decorative papers
- scissors
- toilet paper roll
- glue
- googly eyes
- decorative trim

Instructions:

1. For fancy noisemakers, follow the template below to trace and cut out two paper circles. Cut slits at the dotted lines, and then bend the fringed ends down.

2. Glue one paper circle around one end of the toilet paper roll so that the fringed paper goes around the entire outside edge. Put googly eyes in the tube, and then seal the other end with the other paper circle the same way.

3. Decorate the outside of the tube with colorful paper and trim. Don't forget to add googly eyes! Now make some noise!

Template

Eye Win!

Nothing says "winner" like a giant eye! With these eye-catching award ribbons, you can reward anyone for a job well done!

Keep Your Eyes Peeled

It's definitely more fun to eat your veggies when they're smiling back at you! Just use tape to make faces on your food—felt smiles are optional!

A Key to the Problem

Just add a colorful key cover and a pair of googly eyes, and you'll never lose sight of a key again!

Butterflies with Eyes

It's a bird... It's a plane... It's a...butterfly?
Give your googly eyes wings—and a clip, so they can sparkle anywhere!

Supplies needed:
- craft wire
- fabric
- pencil
- scissors
- glue
- small clothespins
- googly eyes

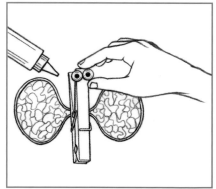

Instructions:

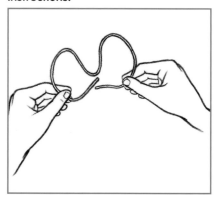

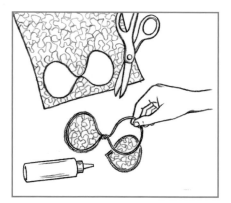

1. Twist a 6" piece of wire into a sloping M shape, curving the end pieces back into the center to create wings.

2. Wrap the end pieces into a tight coil in the center. Lay the wings on a piece of fabric, trace the outline, and cut the fabric to fit the wire. Glue the fabric to the wings.

3. Glue the wings to the underside of the clothespin with the fabric pattern faceup. Glue googly eyes to the top of the clothespin, and allow it to dry.

GAGA TIP
You can also find a butterfly patch, and glue it on a clothespin with eyes.

B-Eye-N-G-O

Ready for an eye-popping game?
Use googly eyes as markers for your next bingo game!

B	I	n	G	O
5	29	●	10	3
●	2	●	24	28
4	26	●	23	30
15	14	●	22	●
13	●	●	18	11

B	I	n	G	O
21	16	4	15	30
11	8	1	28	29
19	27	FREE!	18	25
17	26	6	12	7
9	5	24	14	2

Oooo...Look!

Draw attention to the matter. To make this eye-catching magnet, glue two eyes to a magnetic strip, between an L and a K. Now the most important thing on your refrigerator is sure to get a look!

Full of Hot Air

Q: What do you say when a balloon pops?
A: "May you rest in pieces!"

Balloons are people too. Well, maybe not, but you can make them look like people if you add googly eyes and draw some funny faces!

Supplies needed:
- balloons
- permanent markers
- googly eyes
- glue
- scissors
- craft foam
- felt
- ribbon

Instructions:

1. Blow up a balloon, and tie it off. Draw a face with a permanent marker. Glue on googly eyes.

2. Cut a 10" x 2" strip of craft foam, and glue one end to the other to make a ring. This will be the base for your balloon.

3. Decorate the base with more foam, felt, ribbon, or other decorations. Set your balloon on the base, and display it with pride!

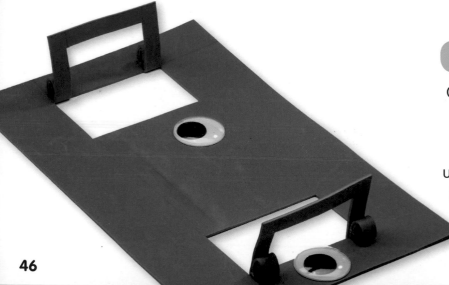

Eye vs. Eye

Can't see eye-to-eye with someone? Forget your differences, and play a game of table hockey with googly eyes as the game pieces. You can use posterboard or foam to make the playing field and your fingers as the hockey sticks!

Create an "Eyesore"

Create your own eyesore by gluing googly eyes to a bandage.

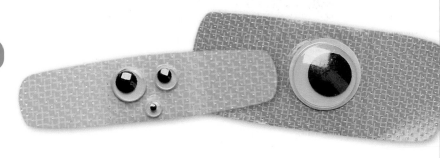

"X" Marks the Spot

Got a treasure to hide?
Decorate a shoe box with an old map, a pirate flag, and a trail of googlies.
Stash yer treasure here, matey!

Pistachio Nut Ladybugs

Add some paint and googly eyes to pistachios to make your own ladybugs that won't fly away!

Blank Faces

Glue eyes on these blank face templates or trace them on paper to create your own different characters!

GAGA TIP
Get creative! Add freckles using sand, make mustaches with feathers, create glasses or crazy hair from pipe cleaners, or anything else you can think of!